PRAISE FOR W[...]

When my kids were little, it was easy to find meaningful resources for studying God's Word, but as they hit the tween years, it became increasingly difficult to find age-appropriate studies to help them connect with others while reflecting on the Word and its power in their lives. *What to Wear* fills that void in every way possible. Catherine Parks uses a casual, informed voice that appeals to kids and parents alike as she points children to the Bible and a deeper understanding of godly character. My kids appreciate the practical ideas for applying and practicing each quality, and I love that Parks gives just the right amount of detail as she guides older children to delight in what we get to "wear" as His followers.

Amber O'Neal Johnston
Author of *A Place to Belong*

Teaching our kids how to walk in step with the Spirit is a critical aspect of raising the next generation. This resource is a creative, biblical, and age-appropriate tool that helps families and churches teach the truth of Colossians 3. Catherine Parks offers a faithful guide in helping kids understand what it looks like to step into their Christian faith, putting off worldliness and putting on virtue. You'll want this Bible study for your family, your homeschool group, and your children's ministry program!

Daniel Darling
Director of the Land Center for Cultural Engagement; bestselling author of *The Characters of Christmas* and *Spiritual Gifts: What They Are and How to Use Them*; coauthor of *The Biggest, Best Light*

In *What to Wear*, Catherine Parks offers middle grade kids a gospel-rich study they can easily access, genuinely enjoy, and meaningfully apply. My favorite part is Catherine's approach to application. She allows Jesus' example to settle into her young readers' minds and then engages their imagination with age-appropriate scenarios that invite them to consider, "How can I 'put on' this Christlike quality?" I know this eight-week study will truly serve my young brothers and sisters in Christ, and I am eager to recommend it to the eight- to twelve-year-olds in my life!

Caroline Saunders
Author of teen Bible studies *Better than Life: How to Study the Bible and Like It* and *Good News: How to Know the Gospel and Live It*

Delightful and full of depth—*What to Wear* is the study companion our kids need right now. It is an engaging discipleship resource that not only offers practical application for the "put off, put on" passages of Colossians but also teaches kids how to rightly divide the Word.

Jamie Erickson
Homeschool mom of five, cohost of the *Mom to Mom Podcast*, and author of *Homeschool Bravely*

WHAT TO WEAR

A KIDS BIBLE STUDY ON

LOOKING LIKE JESUS

CATHERINE PARKS

MOODY PUBLISHERS

CHICAGO

Edited by Amanda Cleary Eastep
Interior design: Paul Nielsen, Faceout Studios
Cover design: Faceout Studio, Spencer Fuller
Cover illustration of sandals copyright © 2022 by Magicleaf / Shutterstock (2074850419). All rights reserved.

Printed by: Versa Press in East Peoria, IL, January 2023

ISBN: 978-0-8024-2887-5

Originally delivered by fleets of horse-drawn wagons, the affordable paperbacks from D. L. Moody's publishing house resourced the church and served everyday people. Now, after more than 125 years of publishing and ministry, Moody Publishers' mission remains the same—even if our delivery systems have changed a bit. For more information on other books (and resources) created from a biblical perspective, go to www.moodypublishers.com or write to:

Moody Publishers
820 N. LaSalle Boulevard
Chicago, IL 60610

1 3 5 7 9 10 8 6 4 2

Printed in the United States of America

CONTENTS

WHAT TO EXPECT

Have you ever had to wear something that felt uncomfortable? Maybe an itchy sweater or shoes that hurt your feet? I don't know about you, but I want to feel good in the clothes I wear. I like things that feel comfortable and that fit with who I am. I'm guessing you might feel the same way. Over the next eight weeks, we will talk about the "clothes" we get to put on as followers of Jesus. As you'll see, they're not really clothes, but that's what Paul, the writer of Colossians, uses to explain how we should live as Christians.

In the New Testament (the second part of the Bible), there's a letter to a church in a town called Colossae (a city in the country that is now Turkey). Paul wrote this letter to encourage the Christians in Colossae. In Colossians 3, Paul tells the church that their identity is now in Christ, and they need to "dress the part," or behave the way a follower of Jesus should. So, there are things they need to "take off," and there are other things they need to "put on." This list of things to put on is not just for the Colossians, but for all who follow Christ, including kids.

What to Wear is an eight-part study of the items of "clothing" below and how we can put them on:

Compassion

Kindness

Humility

Gentleness

Patience

Forbearance and forgiveness

Love

More than that, though, it's a study of how Jesus perfectly fulfilled the requirement to put those things on and how He can help us do it every day.

Each week we will study what it looks like to put on godly character. The first week is a little different than the others. We will discover what we're supposed to take off when we follow Jesus. In weeks 2–8, we will look at the rest of the verses in our passage in Colossians, adding one good character trait each week. Then we will learn about a time when Jesus showed us what that godly character trait looks like.

You will have the chance to draw pictures, write stories, and answer questions about the verses you read. As you go, you will see how you can put on the qualities you're learning about. My prayer is that you will see that the Bible is "living and effective" (Hebrews 4:12), and that studying it can be fun and fulfilling. Along the way, you will hopefully learn more about Jesus and His love for you. And I pray that learning about His love will help you to love Him and others more. After all, the end of our passage says that it's love that we should put on most of all. Let's dive in together!

Note to readers: I used the Christian Standard Bible version, and that's what the fill-in-the-blank questions are taken from. If you don't have that version, ask an adult to help you find one online.

WHAT *NOT* TO WEAR

YOUR SUPERSUIT

Picture a superhero. It could be one you have read about or seen on TV, or it could be one you invent in your imagination.

What does that superhero wear?

_____

_____

How does his or her clothing fit with the name he or she goes by?

_____

_____

_____

A superhero's clothes should match his or her identity. Spiderman *looks* like Spiderman because of his suit, and his suit allows him to act like Spiderman. The clothes he wears fit who he is. We are going to learn that a Christian's "clothes" should also fit who they are . . . sort of.

See, when we talk about "clothes" in this study, we don't mean what we actually wear. The clothes we're going to talk about are not made of cloth. They're not things we can put on our bodies. They're not even things we can touch. But they *are* real.

The book of Colossians in the Bible is a letter to a church in a town called Colossae.

Find Colossians 1:1–2 in your Bible. Read it and answer the questions below:

Who wrote this letter?

_____

Who did they write it to?

_____

_____

How do the writers describe the people they're writing to?

_____

_____

We will learn more about this church tomorrow. *But for now, check the end of verse 2. Fill in the blanks below with the greeting that Paul and Timothy send to the church at Colossae:*

"_____ to you and _____ from _____

our _____ ."

We can tell that Paul and Timothy love these Christians in the Colossian church. They want them to grow in their faith and to know God's grace and peace.

That is my hope for you as you go through this study. I pray that you will grow in grace and peace, and that you will know how much your Father God loves you. I also pray that you will learn more about your identity in Christ and how to wear the "clothes" that match that identity.

Take a moment to pray the prayer below. Ask God to help you grow through this study:

> *Father, I want to understand Your Word, the Bible. I want to grow in grace and peace, and I want to learn about having my identity in You. Please help me grow closer to You as I study my Bible. I love You. Amen.*

ONE BIG HAPPY FAMILY

Yesterday we learned that Paul (and Timothy) wrote a letter to the Colossian church. The people in this church were new Christians. Some of them already knew about God because they were Jews. They had studied and learned the Old Testament. But now they were Christians because they believed Jesus is God's Son and that He had died and been raised again back to life. Others were learning about God for the first time because they had followed false gods and worshiped idols. Yet all of them had come together to follow Jesus and live their lives for Him.

Can you think of any reasons why it might have been hard for the people in this church to get along with each other?

_____

_____

_____

The church is supposed to be a family, but some of these people were very different from each other. Some were rich; others were poor. Some knew a lot about God's Word; others didn't. They ate different foods and wore different clothes. If they focused on those differences, they would never become a family.

Why is it sometimes hard to get along with people who are different from us?

_____

_____

_____

The people in the Colossian church were family because they were all following Jesus, and their sins had been forgiven by God so they could be part of His family.

Before we learn about our identity as Christians, we need to know that we are part of God's family. Have you ever trusted Jesus with your life? You can join God's family right now, and once you're in His family, you'll always be His child. The Bible says God made all things good, but humans have disobeyed His good rules for living. This is called sin, and sin separates us from God because He is perfect and holy.

But Jesus came to make a way for us to be in God's family. He took the punishment we deserve for our sin and paid for it by dying on a cross so that we don't have to be punished. And then He rose again from the grave and went to heaven where He is making things ready for every-one who is part of that family to be together with Him one day. So, even though we disobey God every day, we can be forgiven because Jesus bought our forgiveness with His death.

If you haven't joined God's family, you can talk to Him now:

- *Tell Him you know you're a sinner and you're sorry for disobeying Him.*

- *Thank Him for sending Jesus so that you can be forgiven and saved from the punishment all human beings deserve.*

- *Tell Him you want to live for Him and share His love with others.*

- *Thank Him for saving you and making you part of His family.*

If you are already part of God's family, take a minute to stop and thank Him again for saving you and making you part of His family.

YOUR NEW IDENTITY

Let's review what we have learned so far: The book of Colossians is a letter from Paul (with encouragement from Timothy) to the church at Colossae. This church was a family of Christians from different backgrounds, and they needed to learn how to be a closer family.

Today, we're going to talk about identity. Remember when you thought of your superhero on Day 1? We talked about how a superhero's clothes should match their identity. Identity is just a word for who someone truly is.

In chapter 3 of Colossians, Paul tells the people in this church that their identity (who they are) has changed because they are now following Jesus. Their differences are not as important anymore because they have a new identity.

Read verses 1–4 below:

> So if you have been raised with Christ, seek the things above, where Christ is, seated at the right hand of God. Set your minds on things above, not on earthly things. For you died, and your life is hidden with Christ in God. When Christ, who is your life, appears, then you also will appear with him in glory.

In verse 1, Paul says we should seek the things _____ . Why?
(Hint: It's in the very next words.) Because _____ is there.
In verse 2, he says, "Set your _____ on things _____ ."

Unlike earthly things, the things that are above will never break or fade away. What do you think some of the "things above" are?

_____

_____

In verse 3, Paul tells the people that they have died, and their life is now _____ with Christ in God. But they haven't died . . . he's writing them a letter, so they're still alive. What do you think he means?

_____

_____

Paul wrote these things to the Christians in Colossae so that they would know that their old lives had to die so they could live their new lives in Jesus. This doesn't mean their bodies had to die. But they had to say goodbye to the old way that they lived—the way that didn't fit with their new identity.

For some of the Colossians, the old way they lived included worshiping idols and living in very sinful ways. For others, the old way of life meant trusting in themselves for salvation. They thought they could try to choose the right actions and live the right way and that would be enough to go to heaven with God.

Are there any things that you need to say goodbye to if you are now following Jesus? What do you think they are?

_____

_____

Tomorrow we will learn about some of the thoughts and actions the Colossians needed to "take off," or say goodbye to. Many of them are the same things we still need to take off almost two thousand years later.

Take a minute to pray:

> *Jesus, thank You for being the Messiah—the Promised One who came to save us. Please help me set my mind on things above and not get caught up in things that don't matter. Help me say goodbye to things that don't fit with my new identity. Thank You for loving me. Amen.*

OUT WITH THE OLD

So far this week, we have learned that the Colossians were a group of Christians from different backgrounds who were learning to be a family and to follow Jesus together. They said goodbye to their old lives and identities because they had changed.

And because who they were had changed, they need to "dress" to fit their new identity. So, Paul uses the idea of clothes to help the people in this church understand. He gives them a list of things to take off and put on.

This list is not just for the Colossians, but for everyone who follows Jesus. Paul uses clothes to give us a picture. What he really means is that what we do should reflect who we really are. And if we have trusted in Jesus for salvation and hope, then who we really are is followers of Him.

Read Colossians 3:8–10 below:

But now, put away all the following: anger, wrath, malice, slander, and filthy language from your mouth. Do not lie to one another, since you have put off the old self with its practices and have put on the new self. You are being renewed in knowledge according to the image of your Creator.

Finish writing each of the traits or behaviors listed in verses 8 and 9:

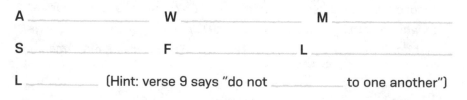

A _____ W _____ M _____

S _____ F _____ L _____

L _____ (Hint: verse 9 says "do not _____ to one another")

Did you notice that these are all things that hurt other people? The Colossians had to take them off so they could be a family and love each other. And we need to take them off too!

On the figure below, draw the most ridiculous, disgusting outfit you can imagine. Think of something you would never wear in public and draw it.

Here are some definitions to help you understand the list of traits better:

Anger: a strong feeling of displeasure that might make you want to hurt someone[1]

Wrath: great anger that expresses itself in a desire to punish someone[2]

Malice: a desire to inflict injury, harm, or suffering on another[3]

Slander: making false and damaging statements about someone[4]

Filthy language: hurtful or gross words meant to harm someone else

Lying: telling someone something that isn't true

1. Cambridge Dictionary, s.v. "anger," https://dictionary.cambridge.org/us/dictionary/english/anger.

2. Vocabulary.com, s.v. "wrath," https://www.vocabulary.com/dictionary/wrath.

3. Dictionary.com, s.v. "malice," https://www.dictionary.com/browse/malice.

4. Cambridge Dictionary, s.v. "slander," https://dictionary.cambridge.org/us/dictionary/english/slander.

Which ones are the hardest for you to take off?

_____

_____

_____

Can you think of examples of stories you've read or seen where one of these things hurt someone?

_____

_____

_____

How do these things change our relationships with other people?

_____

_____

_____

Now, around the edge of your picture, write the words you listed above. This picture is a little silly, but hopefully it will remind you that these things Paul says to take off are not the characteristics you want to wear or display in your life.

Pray and ask God to help you take off the old things and put on the new ones:

Father God, I don't want to wear these gross things. When I'm struggling with anger or lying or other things from the list, please help me remember this picture. Help me remember that I don't want to wear these things and help me take them off and put on Your good clothes instead. I definitely need Your help with that. Thank You for promising to keep working on me. Amen.

WE ALL NEED A HELPER

Have you ever tried to do something that seemed impossible? What was it?

_____

_____

_____

Taking off the old things and putting on the new can feel impossible at times.

As we go on through this study and look at what we *should* wear, we need to remember that we're going to mess up. We will forget our new identity and will put on the old clothes again. Jesus was the only perfect, sinless person who ever lived. Until we're with Him, we will never be without sin.

But God has given us the Holy Spirit to help us. We can't take these things off on our own, but we can ask Him for help each time we face a new challenge.

Jesus never sinned, but just like putting on our dirty "clothes," He took our sin on Himself and took our punishment for that sin. He's the One who gives us the new clothes we're going to learn about in the coming weeks.

Who is the Holy Spirit?

Before Jesus died, He told His friends that it was good that He was going away because when He did, the Helper would come to them. After Jesus went back to heaven, His friends waited for this Helper. It was the Holy Spirit, God's Spirit sent to live in everyone who trusts in Him and becomes part of His family. Sometimes the Holy Spirit is also called the "Comforter" because the Spirit reminds us of how much God loves us. The Spirit helps us understand the Bible and obey God's good rules for our lives. And the Spirit helps us remember to stay close to Jesus.

And, as we put on the new clothes God has for us, it makes the old ones look even worse. The things we get to put on that fit our new identity are listed in the verses below.

As you read this passage, underline each character quality in Colossians 3:12–14 you think we're going to learn to put on.

Therefore, as God's chosen ones, holy and dearly loved, put on compassion, kindness, humility, gentleness, and patience, bearing with one another and forgiving one another if anyone has a grievance against another. Just as the Lord has forgiven you, so you are also to forgive. Above all, put on love, which is the perfect bond of unity.

Take a minute to pray:

Father God, thank You for sending Jesus, who took all our sinful "clothes" onto Himself and died in our place so we can put on our new identity as Christians. Please help us take off the old clothes and dress for our new identity. Thank You for sending the Holy Spirit to help us each day. Please help us live in unity and peace with each other today. Amen.

PUT ON COMPASSION

I FEEL YOUR PAIN

It had happened every day that week, and today was just the same. When Austin's class entered the lunchroom, Juan put down his lunchbox and walked away to get a cup of water. When he returned, his lunchbox had been moved to an empty table. Kids looked on, snickering as he went to sit by himself. Every time it happened, Austin felt sick to his stomach. He knew what the kids were doing was wrong, but some of the ones doing it were his friends. He felt bad for Juan, who hadn't been at the school very long and was still learning English. But what could he do?

We will talk about Austin's situation later in the week and will find out how putting on compassion can help him.

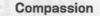 **Compassion**
deeply feeling the suffering of others and taking action to help[5]

Have you ever felt like Austin? Or have you ever been treated like Juan? What did it feel like?

_____

_____

Remember from last week the list of things we are supposed to "put on" when we become followers of Jesus? Let's read Colossians 3:12–14 again:

Therefore, as God's chosen ones, holy and dearly loved, put on compassion, kindness, humility, gentleness, and patience, bearing with one another and forgiving one another if anyone has a grievance against another. Just as the Lord has forgiven you, so you are also to forgive. Above all, put on love, which is the perfect bond of unity.

Did you notice that before Paul gives the list, he tells the Colossians (and us!) three things about who we are. What are those things?

We are:

1. God's _____

2. H _____

3. D _____ L _____

How does that list make you feel?

_____

_____

Remember all those things we're supposed to take off from the last lesson? Those gross things don't belong anymore because of our new identity. God has chosen us to be part of His family. He has called us "holy," which means we are set apart for His mission—a mission to love Him and love others with His love. And He says *we* are loved. Isn't that great news?!

This week we will look at a time when Jesus showed compassion. Learning from Him will help us understand how we can put on compassion. He is our example, and He's also our Savior.

Take a minute to pray:

> *Father, thank You for calling me "chosen," "holy," and "loved." I don't always feel that way, but I know You would not say it if it wasn't true. Help me remember those things when I'm sad or having a hard time. Please help me grow in compassion this week as I learn more about Your compassion for me. Amen.*

---

5. "Understanding the Meaning of Compassion," Compassion, https://www.compassion.com/child-development/meaning-of-compassion/.

TOO TIRED TO CARE?

Find Mark 6 in your Bible.

Before you start reading, you need to know what happened prior to this verse because it was something pretty horrible. John the Baptist, Jesus' cousin and friend, had been put to death by King Herod.

What does repent mean?

Jesus often told people they needed to repent. This word means to turn around and go in the opposite direction. Jesus was saying we all need to stop walking toward sin and instead turn around and walk in God's direction. We need to know that He is better than anything else!

Before that (at the beginning of Mark 6), Jesus had gone back to His hometown, Nazareth. But the people in Nazareth were offended by Him. They recognized Him as the carpenter who had grown up there. Because they didn't think He was anyone special, they didn't want to listen when He told them to repent and believe. So, He left and went to other villages.

Then in Mark 6:7–13, Jesus sent His twelve disciples out to cast out demons and heal the sick and call people to turn away from their sins and believe in Him.

That's a lot for Jesus and His disciples to deal with. How do you think they were feeling?

_____

_____

_____

Read Mark 6:30–31

The disciples (or "apostles") came to Jesus to tell him what had happened when they were away. What did He tell them to do in verse 31?

"Come _____ by yourselves to a remote place and _____ for a while."

Read Mark 6:32–33

What happened when they took a boat to a remote place? ("Remote" means it's away from the city and crowds.)

_____

Do you think they were able to rest? _____

Read Mark 6:34

When Jesus got out of the boat, He saw the crowd. This verse says He had _____ on them. Why? "Because they were like _____ without a _____ ."

We will find out more about the compassion Jesus showed people in this story, and we will learn what He meant about sheep without a shepherd.

But for now, let's remember the definition of compassion from the beginning of this lesson: deeply feeling the suffering of others and taking action to help.

So far in this story, how has Jesus shown compassion?

_____

Do you think it's always easy to show compassion? _____

I bet the disciples were not too excited to get to their "remote" place to rest and find a huge crowd waiting for them. But Jesus shows us that having compassion is possible even when we may not feel like it.

Take a minute to ask God for help:

> *Father, please help me have compassion on other people today, even when I may not feel like it. Thank You for having compassion on me and loving me. Amen.*

WANTED: A GOOD SHEPHERD

Yesterday, we read in Mark 6:34 that Jesus had compassion on the crowds because they were like _____ without a _____.

Tomorrow we will get back to our story in Mark 6, but today we are going to learn more about sheep and shepherds.

What is a shepherd's job?

_____

_____

_____

What do you think happens to sheep who don't have a shepherd?

_____

_____

_____

Read John 10:11

"I am the good shepherd. The good shepherd lays down his life for the sheep."

What does Jesus call Himself in this verse?

_____

What does He say the good shepherd does?

_____

What do you think it means for the shepherd to "lay down his life"?

_____

_____

A good shepherd guides sheep to safety, makes sure they are fed, and protects them from predators. The sheep learn to listen to their shepherd's voice and to follow him. He loves his sheep and is willing to sacrifice himself for them.

Jesus laid down His life on the cross for us, His sheep. He is truly a Good Shepherd. This means we can trust Him because we know He really loves us and does what is best for us.

Take a minute to thank Jesus for being your shepherd:

> *Jesus, thank You for being my shepherd. I would be lost without You. Help me trust You and follow You. Thank You for being a Good Shepherd and laying down Your life for me. I love You. Amen.*

A COMPASSIONATE MIRACLE

Today we're going back to Mark 6 to learn the rest of the story. Remember, Jesus and the disciples had gone in a boat to a remote place, but a huge crowd met them there. Jesus had compassion on the people because they were like sheep without a shepherd. Let's see what He did.

Read Mark 6:34

At the end of the verse, it says He began to _____ *them many things.*

We learned yesterday that sheep listen to their shepherd's voice, and he leads them. Here is Jesus, the Good Shepherd, teaching His sheep with His voice.

He must have taught them for a long time because verse 35 says that "when it grew late," the disciples came to Jesus and told Him to send the people away so they could get something to eat. There were no stores or restaurants in that remote place, and the people would be hungry after listening to Jesus teach all day.

Read Mark 6:37

What does Jesus say to the disciples?

" _____ "

The disciples are confused. They ask if they should go buy enough bread for the people, which would cost as much money as it would take someone two hundred days to earn. That was a lot of money because there were a lot of people there listening to Jesus.

Jesus had compassion on these people. He didn't want to send them away so they could get food. He had a better plan.

Read Mark 6:38

Jesus asked the disciples how much food they had, and they went to find out. When they came back, they reported that they had _____ loaves and _____ fish.

Does that seem like enough food to feed all the people? _____

What do you think the disciples were thinking?

_____

_____

Read Mark 6:39–42

What did Jesus do with the loaves and fish?

_____

_____

Was it enough to feed all the people? (Hint: read verse 42) _____

Read Mark 6:43 and 44

How much food was left over after feeding the people?

_____

How many men ate the food that day? _____

At the time that this was written, crowds like this were counted by the number of men. So, even though it says there were five thousand, we know there were many more people since there were also women and children. That makes this already amazing miracle even more incredible!

Jesus took the food the disciples had in His hands, He prayed, and He performed an amazing miracle. His compassion for the people was heartfelt—He loved them deeply. Because of that love, He taught them and fed them, and later He would die for them and for us.

Compassion isn't always comfortable, and it isn't always convenient. It doesn't mean just *feeling* pity for people. Jesus didn't look at the people, feel bad for them, and then sail away. No, compassion means action. It means feeling someone else's pain so deeply that we join them in it and do what we can to help make it better.

How do you think the people in the crowd felt after this experience?

_____

_____

_____

Take a minute to pray:

Jesus, thank You for showing compassion. Thank You for caring for me. You give me food and clothes and a place to live, and You also gave me the Bible so I will know Your voice and be able to follow You. Help me show the same kind of compassion to other people. Amen.

PUTTING ON COMPASSION

Yesterday we talked about how compassion isn't always comfortable or easy. Compassion isn't just feeling bad for someone and then walking away. That's pity.

Compassion means that we feel someone else's pain enough to do something to help make it better. Jesus was sad about John the Baptist being killed, and He was looking for time alone with the disciples. It wasn't easy or convenient for Him to take all day to teach a crowd and then feed thousands of people. But He did it because He loved them.

Later, Jesus showed even greater compassion. In fact, He showed the greatest love anyone can show.

Read John 15:13

In this verse, Jesus told the disciples, "No one has _____
_____ than this: to _____ _____ his life for his friends."

Remember when we read about the shepherd and the sheep, and Jesus said the good shepherd "lays down his life" for the sheep?

When Jesus died on the cross, He was laying down His life for His friends. He came to feel our sadness and sickness and to take our sin on the cross so that we could know true joy and peace and love.

But, like we talked about earlier in our study, Jesus didn't stay dead! When Jesus rose from the dead and went back up into heaven, He gave us the Holy Spirit to help and guide us to hear His voice. We can't put on compassion on our own; we need His help. And He has promised to give it to us.

Let's read Austin's story again:

It had happened every day that week, and today was just the same. When Austin's class came into the lunchroom, Juan put down his lunchbox and walked away to get a cup of water. When he returned, his lunchbox had been moved to an empty table and the kids looked on, snickering as he went to sit by himself. Every time, Austin felt sick. He knew what they were doing was wrong, but some of the kids doing it were his friends. He felt bad for Juan, who hadn't been at the school very long and was still learning English. But what could he do?

Write an ending for this story based on what you've learned about compassion this week:

In each week of this study, you will add an item of clothing to another drawing to show the different things we are learning to "put on." *Today, on the figure here, draw any article of clothing on the person (a shirt, pants/shorts, a skirt, etc.).*

On that article of clothing, write "compassion."

Apply it

Talk through these questions with an adult, a sibling, or a friend:

- What have you learned about Jesus this week?

- How has Jesus shown compassion to you?

- What have you learned about true compassion from the story about Jesus feeding all those thousands of people? (Is it just a feeling we have toward people, or does it require action?)

- How do you want to grow in compassion? Are there any situations in your life where God might be calling you to put on compassion?

Pray about it

Think about a time when you could have shown compassion to someone but didn't. Tell God about it, ask His forgiveness, and thank Jesus for being compassionate toward you. Then, ask Him to help you, by the Holy Spirit, to put on compassion. Be specific: Ask for help with certain people or situations you're facing. Ask Him to give you an opportunity to put on compassion this week.

Practice it

How can you put on compassion this week? Here are some ideas, but feel free to think of your own!

- Help serve at a local food pantry or other ministry to people with needs for food and clothing.

- Have a yard sale or a lemonade stand to raise money for a family in need or an organization that helps people in your community or around the world.

- Ask an adult to help you research a prison ministry that allows you to send care packages and letters to prisoners. Make this a family project.

- Ask God for an opportunity to share the good news about Jesus with someone this week. Each person's greatest need is to believe in Jesus for salvation.

PUT ON KINDNESS

WHAT IS TRUE KINDNESS?

Alex and Camryn were finally setting up their lemonade stand now that the weather was warm enough. They needed $35 more to buy the video game system they had been saving for. They were taping up their sign when they looked over and saw a tow truck pulling into their neighbor's driveway. As the driver got out and started hooking the tow cables to their neighbor's car, Alex and Camryn looked at each other. They knew their neighbor had lost her job a few weeks earlier. And now she wouldn't be able to drive. They went back to taping up their sign, but suddenly their excitement over lemonade and video games was not quite as strong.

We will talk about Alex and Camryn's situation later in the week and will find out how putting on kindness can help them.

Kindness
speaking and acting with goodness that
meets other people's needs[6]

Have you ever worked hard and saved up for something you wanted? What was it? _____

Do you know anyone like this neighbor who is going through a hard time? Or have you and your family ever gone through a time like that? Describe it below: _____

_____

_____

6. Kindness in "Titus 3:4 Commentary," Precept Austin, https://www.preceptaustin.org/titus_34#kindness%20 chrestotes%20chrestos.

How do you think that feels?

_____

_____

Let's review the list of things in Colossians 3:12–14 that we get to put on when we become followers of Jesus. Fill in the blanks with the quality we've already learned about:

Therefore, as God's chosen ones, holy and dearly loved, put on _____, kindness, humility, gentleness, and patience, bearing with one another and forgiving one another if anyone has a grievance against another. Just as the Lord has forgiven you, so you are also to forgive. Above all, put on love, which is the perfect bond of unity.

Do you remember the three things about our new identity that we learned last week?

We are:

1. God's _____

2. H _____

3. D _____ L _____

Last week we learned about putting on heartfelt compassion. This week we get to learn about kindness, and we will learn about a time when Jesus taught what true kindness is. He is the best example of kindness, but He also helps people to be kind.

Who is a kind person in your life?

_____

What have they done to show kindness to you?

_____

_____

Take a minute to pray and thank God for His kindness and for the person you wrote about above. Write their name into your prayer below:

Father God, thank You for showing kindness to me. Thank You also for _____ , who is kind to me. Please help me understand what it means to put on kindness. Amen.

THE BEST KIND OF NEWS

Today and tomorrow, you will read about a time when Jesus told a story to help people understand what it means to truly love God and other people.

Read Luke 10:25–27

Verse 25 says that an expert in the law came to "test" Jesus. This man had studied the law and wanted to see how much Jesus really knew. The "law" mentioned here is the "law of Moses," or the commandments that God gave to His people in the Old Testament (especially what we know as the Ten Commandments).

What did the man ask Jesus? "Teacher, what must I do to inherit e _____ l _____ ?"

Jesus answered the man's question with a different question. He asked the man what the law said.

The man responded by quoting two verses: Deuteronomy 6:5 and Leviticus 19:18. Both verses were very important for God's people.

Fill in the blanks of the verses below:

"Love the Lord your _____ with all your _____ , with all your _____ , and with all your _____ (Deuteronomy 6:5)

And . . .

"Love your _____ as yourself" (Leviticus 19:18).

Read Luke 10:28

Jesus answered the man and said, "You've answered correctly. Do this and you will _____ ."

The man wanted to know how to have eternal life—life that never ends. Tomorrow we will learn why he wasn't quite satisfied with the answer Jesus gave him. But for now, let's look a little deeper at why Jesus' words are both good news and bad news.

Do you think these instructions are easy to follow? Why or why not?

_____

_____

If the way to have eternal life is to love God and others perfectly, then only one person who ever lived should have eternal life. Who is that person? _____

That could be really bad news for us. We have all failed to follow God's rules. But in another one of Paul's letters, the book of Ephesians in the Bible, he writes that God loves us so much and is "rich in mercy," so He offers us His grace through Jesus (see Ephesians 2:1–9).

Grace means a gift we don't deserve. God's gift to us is that Jesus took our sin and was punished in our place by dying on the cross. Because Jesus always loved perfectly, we can exchange our sin for His perfection. And that means we can have the eternal life that the expert in the law asked about.

We don't get eternal life by loving everyone perfectly; if that was the only way, would anyone have eternal life?

Check one: Yes ☐ No ☐

If it was up to us to be perfect, we could never do it. But we can have eternal life by accepting the free gift Jesus offers us.

Thank Jesus for showing you kindness:

> *Jesus, I know I can't earn eternal life, but You already did it for me. Thank You for taking the punishment for my sins so that I can have the amazing gift of life with You forever. I love You. Amen.*

ARE <u>YOU</u> MY NEIGHBOR?

Yesterday, we learned that Jesus answered the question that the expert in the law asked by telling the man he was right. The way to have eternal life is to love God and your neighbor. But the man didn't get the clue Jesus was giving him. He should have thought, "Oh, I can never do that." Let's find out how he responded instead.

Read Luke 10:29

What does this verse tell us about the man? He wanted to _____
himself. He wanted to prove he was doing what he needed to do to have eternal life and be part of God's kingdom.

What did he ask Jesus?

_____

_____

This is a bit like a child being asked to clean her room and responding by asking, "What counts as my room?" She's thinking, *If they don't say my closet, then I don't have to clean that.* She wants to do the smallest amount of work possible instead of serving as much as she can.

By asking, "Who is my neighbor?" the man was saying, "Well, I don't have to love everyone like that; just the people I'm closest to." So, Jesus told a story, or parable, to answer the man's question and to reveal that his heart was not in the right place.

Parable
This is a story with a lesson. Jesus often taught His followers important truths by telling them parables.

Read Luke 10:30–33

Where was the man in the story leaving from? _____

Where was he going? _____

The people listening to this parable knew that the road from Jerusalem to Jericho was dangerous. So, they would not have been surprised at what happened next.

What happened to the man on the road?

_____

_____

Three people saw the man lying on the road. How did they respond?

Priest: _____

_____

Levite: _____

_____

Samaritan: _____

_____

The priest was a descendant (part of the family) of Aaron, Moses' brother. Aaron's descendants (his sons, grandsons, great-grandsons, great-great-grandsons . . . you get the idea) were assigned the jobs for priests in the temple in Jerusalem. They were seen as holy leaders for God's chosen Jewish people. But instead of helping the man, the priest crossed to the other side of the road and passed by.

Next, a Levite passed in the same way on the other side of the road. Levites helped the priests in the temple. So, he was also seen as a holy leader.

Finally, a Samaritan came up. When the people heard Jesus telling this story, they would have been shocked to hear that the Samaritan helped the man. Samaritans and Jews were not friendly with each other. In fact, they hated each other.

Did you notice a familiar word in verse 33? It says the Samaritan had _____ on the man. He felt the man's pain deeply, and that caused him to show kindness.

Tomorrow we will discover more of what kindness means by seeing how the Samaritan treated the man who was robbed and beaten.

But for now, let's think about the word "neighbor." The expert in the law asked Jesus, "Who is my neighbor?" and Jesus told this parable.

What do you think Jesus is saying about who our neighbors are? Are they just the people who live around us?

_____

_____

Do you think the priest and Levite thought of the man on the road as their neighbor? _____

If Jews and Samaritans hated each other, then most of them wouldn't think of their enemies as their neighbors. But the Samaritan did.

Think of someone you wouldn't want to live next door to (a bully, a grumpy aunt from Iowa, or . . .). Write their name (or names) here:

_____

_____

If we're followers of Jesus, we should treat them with the same kindness we should show to those we love and live alongside.

Take a minute to pray:

> *Father God, please help me see people as neighbors. Please fill me with Your love for those around me today. Amen.*

KINDNESS IS KIND OF HARD

Read Luke 10:34–35

What are some of the ways the Samaritan showed kindness to the injured man?

_____

_____

_____

How do his actions fit with our definition of kindness (speaking and acting with goodness that meets other people's needs)?

_____

_____

_____

_____

Do you think it was easy for him to show kindness in this way? Why or why not?

_____

_____

_____

_____

Note: The Samaritan gave the innkeeper two denarii, which is how much money he would have earned for two whole days of work. And, he said he would pay even more if it was needed.

Read Luke 10:36–37

When Jesus finished the story, He asked the expert in the law which of the three men proved to be a neighbor to the man who was robbed. How did the man answer Jesus?

_____

_____

_____

What did Jesus tell him to do?

_____

_____

_____

This was not what the man was expecting. Showing kindness to our neighbors is actually a lot harder than what we might have imagined. The example Jesus gave was a man loving his enemy in the way we might only love a close family member. If this is what it takes to be part of God's kingdom, we're going to need a lot of help.

And that's the good news: He gave us the Holy Spirit to help us show kindness to *our* neighbors, even when it's really hard.

Take a minute to pray:

Father God, please help me show kindness to my neighbors—the ones who live in my house, the ones who live close to me, and the ones who don't live anywhere around me. Please give me Your love for those neighbors who are really hard to love, even the ones who don't love me back. Thank You for promising to help me. Amen.

PUTTING ON KINDNESS

This week we have learned that kindness isn't always easy. Sometimes it costs us a lot to be kind. We might have to give up our time, our money, or our things.

We've also learned that God has commanded us to love Him with every part of ourselves. Do you remember the three things we are supposed to love Him with from Deuteronomy 6:5? (Hint: Look at Day 2.)

1. _____

2. _____

3. _____

We're also supposed to love our neighbors as ourselves. What did you learn about who your neighbors are?

_____

_____

_____

_____

_____

Jesus seems to be saying that our neighbor is anyone who we see in need. It could be someone in our home or someone on the other side of the world. Whoever it is, we should love them and show them kindness. But the good news is that He will help us to be kind. We never have to do it on our own.

Let's read Alex and Camryn's story again:

Alex and Camryn were finally setting up their lemonade stand now that the weather was warm enough. They needed $35 more to buy the video game system they had been saving for. They were taping up their sign when they looked over and saw a tow truck pulling into their neighbor's driveway. As the driver got out and started hooking the tow cables to their neighbor's car, Alex and Camryn looked at each other. They knew their neighbor had lost her job a few weeks earlier. And now she wouldn't be able to drive. They went back to taping up their sign, but suddenly their excitement over lemonade and video games was not quite as strong.

Write an ending for this story based on what you've learned about kindness this week:

_____

_____

_____

_____

_____

_____

_____

_____

_____

_____

_____

Turn to page 35. It's time to draw another item of clothing on your person. On today's article of clothing, write "Kindness."

Apply it

Talk through these questions with an adult, a sibling, or a friend:

- What have you learned about Jesus this week?

- How has Jesus shown kindness to you?

- What have you learned about true kindness from this passage? Who is a "neighbor" you have trouble showing kindness to?

Pray about it

Think about a time when you could have been kind to someone but weren't. Tell God about it, ask His forgiveness, and thank Jesus for showing kindness to you. Then, ask Him to help you, by the Holy Spirit, to put on kindness today. Be specific: Ask for help with certain people or situations you're facing. Ask Him to give you an opportunity to put on kindness this week.

Practice it

How can you put on kindness this week? Here are some ideas, but feel free to think of your own!

- Pray for someone you have a hard time loving.

- Give money or food to someone in need.

- Help a sibling or another family member with a project.

- Ask God for an opportunity to share the good news about Jesus with someone this week. Each person's greatest need is to believe in Jesus for salvation.

PUT ON HUMILITY

THINKING ABOUT ~~ME~~ YOU

> Every Saturday, Henry and Caroline had to do a few chores around their house. One Saturday, Henry was riding his bike and slid on some gravel, wrecking the bike and scraping his knee pretty badly. He limped around the house, telling his parents he couldn't walk to do his chores and suggesting that Caroline could do them. Caroline listened from her room, frustrated. *He always seems to find a way to get out of his chores*, she thought. *It's not fair!*

We will talk about Caroline's frustration later in the week and find out how putting on humility can help her.

Humility

not thinking of yourself as being better or higher than others

Have you ever been frustrated like Caroline? When is a time that you've felt like things aren't fair?

_____

_____

_____

In our passage from Colossians 3, Paul tells the people in the church at Colossae that they should put on humility toward each other. This week we will learn more about humility, and we'll look at a time when Jesus showed humility. Then we can apply what we've learned to Caroline's situation.

Let's review the list of things in Colossians 3:12–14 that we get to put on when we become followers of Jesus. Fill in the blanks with the traits we've already studied:

Therefore, as God's chosen ones, holy and dearly loved, put on
_____ , _____ , humility, gentleness, and
patience, bearing with one another and forgiving one another if anyone has a grievance against another. Just as the Lord has forgiven
you, so you are also to forgive. Above all, put on love, which is the
perfect bond of unity.

Tomorrow we will look at a time when Jesus showed us what humility
looks like. But first, we need to understand what humility is.

When you hear the word "humble," what do you think of?

_____

_____

Read Philippians 2:3–4

Let's see what these verses say about humility. First, we see what
humility is *not*.

Verse 3 says we should not do things out of _____ *ambition
or conceit.*

Oonceit
excessive pride in oneself

According to this verse, what is humility not*?*

_____

_____

*Instead, how should we think of other people? Write the end of verse 3
below:*

_____

_____

_____

Then verse 4 tells us we should not just care about ourselves, but we should also care about other people.

Is it easier for you to think about yourself and what you want, or to think about others and what they want? Check one:

Myself ☐ **Others** ☐

It's easier for all of us to think about ourselves. If we were great at thinking of others, we wouldn't need to be told to put on humility. But just because it's hard doesn't mean it's impossible. We'll learn more about humility and how Jesus can help us this week.

Take a minute to pray:

Father God, it's so easy for me to think about myself and so hard for me to think about others and to care for them the way You do. Please help me understand what it means to put on humility, and help me to be humbler. Amen.

DON'T WORRY, BE HUMBLE

For the next few days, we will read in John 13 about a time when Jesus showed His disciples what humility is.

The night before Jesus died on the cross, He came to a room to have dinner with His twelve disciples. But this wasn't just any dinner. They were having the Jewish Passover dinner.

Read John 13:1

What do you learn about Jesus from this verse? What did He know?

_____

_____

_____

How did He feel about the disciples?

_____

_____

Read John 13:2

What was Judas going to do?

_____

Do you think Jesus knew what Judas was going to do? Why or why not?

_____

_____

_____

What is the Passover?

After God delivered His people from being slaves in Egypt, He instructed them to have a Passover dinner each year to remember the way He had brought them out of slavery. They ate flat bread because the night before they left Egypt, they didn't have time to wait for the yeast in the bread to rise. What no one knew, though, was that the Passover was like a road sign pointing the way to Jesus. God reminded His people of how He had delivered them from slavery to Egypt and now He was going to deliver them from an even greater slavery: slavery to sin.

Now read John 13:3

This verse tells us that Jesus knew three things. What are they?

1. Jesus knew the Father had given _____ into His hands (or under His power).

2. Jesus knew that He had come _____ God.

3. Jesus knew that He was _____ _____ to God.

Tomorrow we will read more and discover how Jesus showed humility to the disciples. But for now, we learn that Jesus was able to show humility because of the three things we listed above. Jesus could serve the people around Him and meet their needs because He knew God the Father was going to take care of Him.

Sometimes we struggle to care about others because we're so worried about ourselves. We think we can't give our money or time or things to other people because we might not have enough left.

But if God is our Father, we can trust that He will take care of us. And when we trust Him to care for us, then we can care for other people.

Take a minute to pray:

Father, sometimes I have a hard time thinking of others because I'm so busy thinking about myself. Help me remember that You take care of me, and You love me. Fill me up with Your love so I can care for the people around me and not just think about myself. Thank You for loving me. Amen.

STINKY FEET

Yesterday we learned that Jesus knew the Father had given everything into His hands and that He was going back to be with the Father. He trusted the Father, and that helped Him to humbly serve others.

We also learned that Jesus was going to be betrayed. Who was going to betray Him? _____

Read John 13:4–5

In the space below, write or draw a picture of what Jesus did:

At that time, people wore sandals and walked on dirty, dusty streets where many animals had been. Their feet were filthy and the job of washing them was usually something done by servants. That helps us understand how Peter reacted in the next verses.

Read John 13:6–8

How does Peter feel about Jesus washing his feet?

_____

_____

How do you think you would feel if Jesus knelt down to wash your stinky feet?

_____

_____

Read John 13:9

In verse 8, Jesus said that if He didn't wash Peter, then Peter would have "no part" with Him. To be part of Jesus' family, Peter needed to be washed clean. We will learn more about this idea tomorrow.

How did Peter respond when Jesus said that? What did he say?

_____

_____

Peter was eager to be washed because he wanted to belong with Jesus. Aren't you thankful that Jesus has made a way for us to be part of His family?

Let's take a minute to pray and thank Him now:

> *Jesus, thank You for being humble. You humbled yourself to wash the disciples' feet, and You humbled Yourself even more to die for me. You took my sin so I would have a way to be part of Your family. Thank You so much for thinking of my needs and caring for me. I love You. Amen.*

WHAT GREATNESS LOOKS LIKE

Today we will discover more about why Jesus washed His disciples' feet and what that has to do with us today.

Read John 13:12–15

What did Jesus say the disciples called Him?

_____

Why do you think they called Him those things?

_____

What did Jesus say the disciples should do?

_____

This was hard for the disciples to hear. They didn't want to see Jesus washing their feet, and they definitely didn't want to wash *each other's* feet. That was too gross.

Jesus knew this would be hard for them to understand. Earlier in His time with them, they had been walking to a town and they were arguing. They thought Jesus didn't hear them, but He knew what they were arguing about. It was about which of them was the greatest (Mark 9:33–36; Luke 9:46–47).

Have you ever argued with a sibling or a friend about who was better at something? What was it about?

_____

_____

It could be who was better at drawing, playing a sport, a school subject, or blowing the biggest bubble. We argue about all kinds of things.

The disciples had argued about who was the greatest, and now Jesus was telling them to put all of that aside and instead to wash each other's feet. He told them that if He, their leader, washed their feet, then they should follow His example. He was showing them what humility looks like.

He wasn't saying, "You all are greater than me, so I'm going to wash your feet." Instead, He was saying, "This is what greatness looks like: humbly serving each other."

Jesus even washed the feet of Judas, the man who would betray Him. Sometimes showing humility means serving even the people who don't love us back. We can't do this in our own strength. We need to ask for God's help to be truly humble.

Let's ask Him now:

Father, some people are easy for me to serve. But with other people, it's really hard. Thank You, Jesus, for showing me what it really means to be great—to be a servant. Help me to be humble and serve other people, even when it's hard. Thank You for serving me. Amen.

PUTTING ON HUMILITY

This week we have learned that humility can be really hard. Sometimes it means doing hard jobs (like washing stinky feet) for people who don't show love and kindness to us.

Can you think of any people in your life who you have a hard time serving? Or can you think of parts of your life—like sports, talents, or schoolwork—in which you want people to see how great you are? Write them here:

_____

_____

Jesus wanted His disciples to know that true greatness isn't making everyone else do what you want them to do. Instead, humility means being willing to do what no one wants to do and doing it out of love without calling attention to yourself.

The following day, Jesus would give us an even greater picture of humility as He took the sin of the world on Himself and died in our place. *That* is true greatness.

Let's read Henry and Caroline's story again:

> Every Saturday, Henry and Caroline had to do a few chores around their house. Today, Henry was riding his bike and slid on some gravel, wrecking the bike and scraping his knee pretty badly. He limped around the house, telling his parents he couldn't walk to do his chores and suggesting that Caroline could do them. Caroline listened from her room, frustrated. *He always seems to find a way to get out of his chores*, she thought. *It's not fair!*

Write an ending for this story based on what you've learned about humility this week:

_____

_____

_____

_____

_____

_____

_____

_____

_____

_____

_____

_____

_____

_____

Turn to page 35. Add another item of clothing to your person. On the new article of clothing, write "Humility."

Apply it

Talk through these questions with an adult, a sibling or a friend:

- What have you learned about Jesus this week?

- How has Jesus shown humility to you?

- What have you learned about true humility from John 13? Who do you need to serve with humility?

Pray about it

Think about a time when you could have been humble, but you weren't. Tell God about it, ask His forgiveness, and thank Jesus for showing humility and serving you. Then, ask Him to help you, by the Holy Spirit, to put on humility today. Be specific: Ask for help with certain people or situations you're facing. Ask Him to give you an opportunity to put on humility this week.

Practice it

How can you put on humility this week? Here are some ideas, but feel free to think of your own!

- Do an act of secret service without anyone else knowing about it, and don't tell them.

- Offer to help someone with a job or chore.

- Look for ways to give the best to others, like the last cookie or first choice of what to watch on TV.

- Ask God for an opportunity to serve others by sharing the good news about Jesus with someone this week. Each person's greatest need is to believe in Jesus for salvation.

PUT ON GENTLENESS

NOT JUST FOR PETS

Cora and Aubrey had been best friends since first grade. When Maddie moved in next door, Cora was excited to introduce her to Aubrey. She knew the three of them would get along and have a lot of fun. But Aubrey kept telling Maddie how she needed to dress and do her hair and talk so she could be part of their "group." When Maddie didn't follow Aubrey's rules, Aubrey ignored her or seemed to be angry. Cora didn't know what to do. She felt bad for Maddie, but she was afraid she might lose Aubrey's friendship if she stood up to her.

We will talk about Cora's situation later in the week, and we'll learn how putting on gentleness can help her.

Gentleness
being meek or lowly;
using our strength and power to lovingly help others[7]

Have you ever felt like Cora? Have you ever known someone who treated people the way Aubrey treated Maddie? What happened?

_____

_____

_____

_____

_____

_____

7. "Ephesians 4:2–3 Commentary," Precept Austin, https://www.preceptaustin.org/ephesians_42-3.

Let's review. List the "clothes" we've learned about in the past few weeks:

Put on:

1. _____

2. _____

3. _____

This week we will study what Jesus had to say about gentleness. What do you think of when you hear the word "gentle"? Write about it or draw a picture of what you see in your mind:

Maybe you think of petting a small animal or holding a baby and hearing someone say, "Be gentle!" We know being gentle means you're not harsh or violent. But you might be thinking, "What does petting an animal have to do with Cora's situation?"

That's a great question! By the end of this week, we will learn that gentleness is a lot more than just the way we hold fragile things.

Read the following verse. On the next page, write what it teaches you about gentleness.

A gentle answer turns away anger,
but a harsh word stirs up wrath. (Proverbs 15:1)

_____

_____

_____

_____

Gentleness is more than just how we talk, but I think everyone would say they would rather be spoken to with gentleness than with anger. And sometimes speaking gentle words can help someone *else* not to be angry.

It's hard for us to be gentle, but we can learn how from Jesus. And, gentleness is one of the fruits of the Spirit mentioned in Galatians 5:22–23. This means it's something that the Holy Spirit helps us to grow in, and that's really good news.

Take a minute to pray:

> *Father, I'm not always gentle. Sometimes my words and my actions are harsh. I need Your help to become gentler. Help me this week to understand what gentleness is and to put it on. Thank You for being gentle with me. Amen.*

ALL RULES, ALL THE TIME

Read Matthew 23:1–2

The scribes and Pharisees were religious leaders for God's people. They wanted people to obey the rules God had given His people after He brought them out of Egypt. God's rules are good, and He gave them to people so they would know the best way to live—the way that leads to happiness and wholeness for everyone.

There was a problem, though.

Read Matthew 23:3

What did the scribes and Pharisees not do?

_____

_____

These leaders told the people to obey the laws, but *they* didn't obey!

Verse 4 tells us the problem was even worse than that.

The scribes and Pharisees had added lots of extra rules that were meant to "help" the people to obey God. Instead of helping, though, these extra rules just put heavy burdens on God's people. It was impossible to keep all these extra rules, and the people were tired.

Has there ever been a time when you felt like you had so much to do that you couldn't possibly do it all? Or maybe a time when you were trying to follow the rules, but you just kept messing up? Write about that time below:

_____

_____

_____

If you've ever felt like that, you can probably understand a little about how the Jewish people felt about all the rules the scribes and Pharisees expected them to obey. It felt impossible!

How did Jesus describe these extra rules in verse 4?

He said the leaders put _____ *on the people.*

Were these things easy or hard to carry? _____

Where did they put these loads? _____

Jesus said these leaders wanted honor, and they did things out of pride. They wanted places of honor, they dressed in ways that made them look extra holy, and they wanted people to treat them like they were very important.

Do you think they truly cared about the people they were leading? _____
Why or why not?

_____

_____

_____

We will learn more about this tomorrow, but how do you think Jesus is different from these leaders?

_____

_____

Let's take a minute to pray and thank Jesus that He is not like these leaders:

Jesus, thank You that You are different from the leaders who put heavy burdens on people. Help me come to You when I feel like what I'm carrying is too hard. Thank You for being a good leader and for loving me with gentleness. Amen.

(THAT'S YOKE, NOT YOLK)

When Jesus came and started preaching and performing miracles, more and more people began to follow Him and listen to His teaching. He was different than the scribes and Pharisees, who we learned about yesterday. He lived a life of kindness and humility, serving people and helping them.

Read Matthew 11:28–30

In Matthew 11, we see that Jesus was not like the scribes and Pharisees. Instead of putting heavy loads on people's shoulders, what did He say? Write Matthew 11:28 below:

_____

_____

Then He told them to take something and put it on. What was it?

_____

What is a yoke?
A yoke is a kind of collar that links two oxen together so they can work to pull a plow. A farmer would use it so the oxen could share the load.

Have you ever had a hard job to do that became easier when someone helped you? Write about it:

_____

_____

_____

_____

The people had been carrying a heavy load, and Jesus told them to come to Him and take up *His* yoke instead. That seems a little strange, but what do we learn about the yoke Jesus gives His followers? *Fill in the blanks with words from verse 30:*

His yoke is _____ *and His burden is* _____ .

The other leaders were making the people suffer under a heavy load, but Jesus said to come to Him instead. He does not make people suffer under extra rules and laws. Instead, He bears the yoke with us and shows us the path to true life and joy.

Tomorrow we will learn more about the yoke that Jesus gives us. But for now, isn't it good news that He wants us to come to Him when we are tired and weary?

Let's thank Him now:

> *Jesus, thank You for inviting me to come to You when I'm weary and when I'm trying to do what's right but I'm failing. Thank You for not giving me a heavy load to carry. Help me remember that obeying You leads to true life and joy. Amen.*

GENTLE ≠ WIMPY

Read Matthew 11:29

How did Jesus describe Himself in this verse? "I am _____
and _____ *."*

Some translations of the Bible use the word "lowly." Another word for "lowly" is "gentle."

On Day 1 of this week, we talked about the word "gentle" and some of the things that it means. Today we will try to understand how Jesus was gentle.

Sometimes when we think of gentleness, we think about someone being weak or wimpy. There's a saying that goes, "She's so gentle, she wouldn't hurt a fly." We might think about a gentle person being quiet and scared.

But that doesn't describe Jesus, does it?

Circle the words below that describe Jesus:

Weak   Powerful   Worried   Strong   Afraid   Wise

I think this is a better definition for the kind of gentleness Jesus showed:

Gentleness
using our strength and power to lovingly help others

How does that definition help you understand Jesus better?

_____

_____

_____

Remember when we talked about a yoke yesterday? In these verses, we get a picture of a weak animal, like an ox, who has been struggling under a heavy load. Then Jesus, like a strong ox, helps the weak one. He shares the load and is gentle with the weaker creature. *If you like to draw, you could draw a picture of Jesus helping you carry something heavy in your life:*

Jesus is our gentle Savior. He doesn't get angry with those who are trying to carry heavy burdens. Instead, He tells them to take off those burdens and to put on His light burden instead. How does that make you feel?

_____

_____

_____

Sometimes it's hard for us to understand why Jesus has a yoke or a burden for us to carry. Wouldn't it be better if we didn't have to carry anything at all?

Have you ever helped an adult or a friend with a big job? How did you feel when you finished your good work?

_____

_____

_____

God created us to glorify Him and enjoy Him. One of the ways we do this is by obeying His laws and doing good work. Jesus knows we are the happiest when we're doing what we were created to do. Just like you feel good when you finish a big school project, we feel good when we're obeying and staying close to Jesus.

But this is super important! We don't obey to earn anything. The Bible says we cannot earn God's love (and that's great news because we would fail!). Instead, He offers it freely. We just get to accept it and walk with Him.

Take a minute and pray:

> *Father, thanks for creating me to glorify and enjoy You. Thank You for giving me good work to do. But I know I'm weak and need Your strength and help to do the work You have for me. Thank You for being gentle and helping me. Help me to stay close to You always. Amen.*

PUTTING ON GENTLENESS

This week we have learned that gentleness isn't weakness. It actually takes a lot of strength to be gentle. Don't you think it's harder sometimes to help other people than it is to boss them around?

Are there any people in your life who you struggle to be gentle with? Maybe you are like Aubrey, and sometimes you want to give people rules and conditions to be your friend. Or maybe you want to be gentle, but your words come out angry and rude sometimes. In the space below, write about how you want to grow in gentleness:

_____

_____

_____

Jesus showed us a better way than what the scribes and Pharisees did. They wanted to *look* holy, but they were really hurting people with all their extra rules. Jesus used His strength to help the people, and He does the same thing for us.

Let's read Cora's story again:

> Cora and Aubrey had been best friends since first grade. When Maddie moved in next door, Cora was excited to introduce her to Aubrey. She knew the three of them would get along and have a lot of fun. But Aubrey kept telling Maddie how she needed to dress and do her hair and talk so she could be part of their "group." When Maddie didn't follow Aubrey's rules, Aubrey ignored her or seemed to be angry. Cora didn't know what to do. She felt bad for Maddie, but she was afraid she might lose Aubrey's friendship if she stood up to her.

Write an ending for this story based on what you've learned about gentleness this week:

Turn to page 35. Add another item of clothing to your person.
On the new article of clothing, write "Gentleness."

Apply it

Talk through these questions with an adult, a sibling, or a friend:

- What have you learned about Jesus this week?

- How has Jesus shown gentleness to you?

- What have you learned about gentleness this week? Who do you need to be gentle with?

Pray about it

Think about a time when you could have been gentle, but you weren't. Tell God about it, ask His forgiveness, and thank Jesus for showing gentleness and serving you. Then, ask Him to help you, by the Holy Spirit, to put on gentleness today. Be specific: Ask for help with certain people or situations you're facing. Ask Him to give you an opportunity to put on gentleness this week.

Practice it

How can you put on gentleness this week? Here are some ideas, but feel free to think of your own!

- Help someone with a task that seems too big for them.

- When you're tempted to put rules on someone (like, "You can play with me if . . ."), instead, put on gentleness. Let them have freedom to do it their way.

- Think of someone who is carrying a heavy burden or who is sad, and write them a letter or send a video to cheer them up.

- Ask God for an opportunity to serve others by sharing the good news about Jesus with someone this week. Each person's greatest need is to believe in Jesus for salvation.

PUT ON PATIENCE

A PATIENT PATIENT

Landon was tired of his hospital room. He was tired of machines beeping and medicine going into his body. He wanted to go home and play outside with other kids and live a normal life. His parents and the doctors kept saying, "Just two more weeks," but that seemed like such a long time. He didn't know why his body had cancer in it, but he was so tired of being sick. He felt like no one else had ever gone through something this terrible.

Have you ever felt like Landon? Maybe you have gone through a really hard time, or you know someone else who has been sick like Landon. Or maybe you're waiting for something, and it feels like it will never happen.

This week we are talking about patience. When you hear the words "Be patient," what do you think of?

_____

_____

_____

_____

_____

Patience
enduring difficult circumstances and being faithful during suffering[8]

8. "Colossians 3:12–14 Commentary," Precept Austin, https://www.preceptaustin.org/colossians_312-25.

Write about a time it was hard for you to be patient:

_____

_____

_____

_____

We will come back to Landon's story later in the week. In the meantime, let's review the list of things we're supposed to put on as followers of Jesus. *Underline each item we've already learned about, listed in Colossians 3:12–14:*

> Therefore, as God's chosen ones, holy and dearly loved, put on compassion, kindness, humility, gentleness, and patience, bearing with one another and forgiving one another if anyone has a grievance against another. Just as the Lord has forgiven you, so you are also to forgive. Above all, put on love, which is the perfect bond of unity.

At the beginning of this lesson, there's a definition of "patience." It includes the word "enduring," which is one of those words we should define so we can better understand what patience really is.

Endure
to bear up or persevere during hardship

This week we will learn about a time when Jesus showed perfect patience during terrible hardship. And He did it for *us*.

Let's thank Him now:

> *Jesus, thank You for Your perfect example of patience. As I study this week, help me understand how much You love me. And help me to love You in return. Amen.*

HE KNOWS OUR PAIN

Jesus gave us a perfect example of patience in the hours leading up to His death on the cross. When He was handed over to be crucified, He didn't just go straight to the cross. Today, we will read about what happened first.

Here's what happened before Jesus was arrested and brought to the Jewish high priest and to the Roman leader, Pilate. Pilate had asked the crowd what should be done to Jesus, and they shouted, "Crucify Him!"

Read Mark 15:16–20

A whole battalion of soldiers came and took Jesus away. Any guesses at how many soldiers were in a battalion? _____ [9] (Some Bibles have little notes at the bottom of the page that give information like this. My notes say a battalion was around six hundred men.)

According to verses 17 and 18, the soldiers did several cruel things to Jesus. List them below:

1. Clothed Him in a _____

2. Twisted together a _____ and put it on Him

3. Saluted Him with the name "_____"

4. Struck His _____ with a _____

5. _____ on Him

6. _____ down to Him to make fun of Him

---

9. "Greek *cohort*; a tenth of a Roman legion, usually about 600 men," *ESV Bible, The Single Column Journaling Edition* (Wheaton, IL: Crossway, 2011), 1115.

WHAT TO WEAR

Has anyone ever made fun of you? How did you feel?

_____

_____

How do you think Jesus felt when the soldiers were mocking Him, spitting on Him, and beating Him?

_____

_____

Sometimes we forget that Jesus felt pain and sorrow, just like we do. But you can be encouraged that He knows what it's like to be made fun of. When you feel angry or sad or embarrassed, He understands. You can go to Him with all those feelings, and He can help you. He's been there, too.

Take a minute to pray:

> Jesus, it's such good news to know that You understand how I feel. I'm sorry You had to suffer and be mocked and beaten. But I'm so thankful You went through that because You love me. Thank You for enduring that for my sake. Amen.

A SILENT RESCUER

Yesterday we learned that Jesus was mocked and beaten before He was crucified. Today we will read about what happened while He was on the cross.

Read Mark 15:21–22

Who do you think the "they" in verse 21 is talking about?

_____

These soldiers took a man named Simon out of the crowd and made him carry the cross for Jesus. The cross was very heavy. They took Jesus to a place called Golgotha.

According to verse 22, what does Golgotha mean?

_____

Read Mark 15:23–32

Draw a picture or describe the scene in the space below:

Two criminals were crucified next to Jesus, one on the left and one on the right. When people walked by, they mocked and taunted Him, telling Him to save Himself even though they didn't believe He actually could. The scribes and priests also mocked Him. All the while, Jesus stayed silent. He didn't respond to their words or actions.

What were the Roman soldiers doing while He was dying? (See verse 24.)

These men didn't care about Jesus at all. They just wanted what they could get from Him while He was dying.

What do you feel when you read this story?

Later in Mark 15, we learn that some of the women who followed Jesus were there when He was crucified. *How do you think they felt while people were mocking Him? What do you think they wanted to do?*

In verse 31, the religious leaders said, "He saved others, but he cannot save himself." But we know that Jesus *could* have saved Himself. Yet He didn't because He was on a rescue mission to save us. And that is very good news for us!

Thank Him now:

Jesus, You suffered so much. Your body was beaten and broken, and people made fun of You. And You went through all this suffering so that You could take the punishment I deserved for my sins. I can never say thank You enough times. But I will say it anyway. Thank You. I love You. Amen.

LOOKING TOWARD VICTORY

Today we will finish the story of Jesus on the cross.

Read Mark 15:33–39

After He suffered for hours on the cross, Jesus cried out to God the Father. Not only was He in terrible physical pain, He was also experiencing the terrible weight of all our sin. This was why He chose to die—to take the punishment we deserved. He was the only perfect One who could pay that price. Then He took His last breath and died.

Some other things happened while He was dying. The sixth hour was noon, and the ninth hour was three o'clock in the afternoon. What happened from noon to 3 p.m.?

_____

_____

After Jesus breathed His last breath, what happened in the temple?

_____

_____

These were signs that Jesus was truly who He said He was—the Son of God. How do you think people at the cross or in the temple would have felt when these things happened?

_____

_____

Read verse 39 again.

Centurions were military officers who oversaw one hundred soldiers in the Roman army. A centurion was at the cross because it was his job, not because he was a follower of Jesus. *But what did he say when Jesus died?*

_____

_____

We read in Luke's account of the crucifixion that, like the centurion, one of the robbers next to Jesus trusted Him while he was dying. Jesus told the robber he would be with Him in paradise.

Hebrews 12:2 says that Jesus endured the pain and shame of the cross because of the joy that waited for Him on the other side. He knew He would soon be victorious over sin and death and would be sitting at the right hand of God.

Thinking about that future joy was what made it possible for Him to be patient while people treated Him so horribly. He was able to endure the terrible pain because He knew victory was coming, and He knew He was making a way for people like the robber, the centurion, and you and me to be with Him forever.

Write your own prayer to Jesus below:

_____

_____

_____

_____

PUTTING ON PATIENCE

This week we have learned that Jesus was patient in suffering. He didn't yell at the people who were beating and mocking Him. He didn't use His power to get down from the cross. He endured because He knew that victory was coming. Jesus knew what waited for Him on the other side of death.

We don't always know what the outcome of our hard circumstances will be. When we're hurt—either our bodies or our feelings—we don't know how things will turn out. But, like Jesus, we can have hope and joy for the future.

Is there anything in your life that feels hard right now? Maybe it's sickness, sadness, or something you really wish would change. Write it here:

_____

_____

_____

Romans 8:28 says: "We know that all things work together for the good of those who love God, who are called according to his purpose."

What happened to Jesus was terrible, and sometimes what happens to us is terrible too. Bad and sad things happen in this broken world where we live. And being patient doesn't mean we have to go through those things silently.

If someone is hurting you, always tell an adult you trust. People who do bad things should not be allowed to go on doing them.

But God can use sad things for our good. And because He died and rose to life again, Jesus has the ultimate victory over even the worst things that happen.

Later in Romans 8, Paul writes that nothing can separate us from God's love. Paul gives a whole list of things, including death, that cannot keep us apart from God. We may not know *how* bad things will turn out for our good, but we *can* know that God will never leave us.

And one day, this world will be made new, and we will live without all the sad and bad things that hurt us now. When we go through hard times, we feel a longing for that future joy when every bad thing will go away, and we will be with Jesus.

Let's read Landon's story again:

> Landon was tired of his hospital room. He was tired of machines beeping and medicine going into his body. He wanted to go home and play outside with other kids and live a normal life. His parents and the doctors kept saying, "Just two more weeks," but that seemed like such a long time. He didn't know why his body had cancer in it, but he was so tired of being sick. He felt like no one else had ever gone through something this terrible.

Write an ending for this story based on what you've learned about patience this week:

_____

_____

_____

_____

_____

_____

_____

_____

_____

_____

Turn to page 35. It's time to draw another item of clothing on your person. On today's article of clothing, write "Patience."

Apply it

Talk through these questions with an adult, a sibling, or a friend:

- What have you learned about Jesus from this passage?

- What have you learned about patience from this passage? Why is it so hard to be patient?

- What is an area in your life where you are struggling to be patient? (Remember, being patient and enduring doesn't mean letting people hurt you.)

Pray about it

Think about a time when you needed to be patient, but you weren't. Ask God to forgive you, and thank Jesus for showing patience and dying for you. Then, ask Him to help you, by the Holy Spirit, to put on patience today. Be specific: Ask for help with certain people or situations you're facing. Ask Him to give you an opportunity to put on patience this week.

Practice it

How can you put on patience this week? Here are some ideas, but feel free to think of your own!

- Come up with a list of things you're thankful for. Add to it each day.

- Write a note to someone else who is going through a hard time.

- When you're sad or angry, practice patience by talking to Jesus about it. He knows everything you're feeling and knows what it's like to suffer. Go to Him in prayer.

- Ask God for an opportunity to serve others by sharing the good news about Jesus with someone this week. Each person's greatest need is to believe in Jesus for salvation.

PUT ON FORBEARANCE AND FORGIVENESS

WHEN THINGS ARE UNBEARABLE

Levi had worked for days on a large LEGO® castle. He placed a sign on his bedroom door that said, "Do Not Enter . . . LEGO Master at work!" He told his little brother, Donovan, not to go in or touch his creation or he would be in big trouble. So, when Levi came back to his room after getting a snack downstairs, he was shocked to discover Donovan standing over his castle, which was broken in several places.

Have you ever had something like this happen to you? Maybe a friend or family member ruined something you worked hard on, or maybe someone made fun of you. Write about your experience below:

This week we're learning about forbearance and forgiveness, two ideas that go hand-in-hand. These are things we need to put on when we're in situations like Levi's.

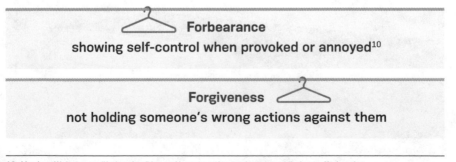

Forbearance
showing self-control when provoked or annoyed[10]

Forgiveness
not holding someone's wrong actions against them

10. *Merriam-Webster*, s.v. "forbearing," https://www.merriam-webster.com/dictionary/forbearing.

We will come back to Levi's story later in the week. *But first, let's review Colossians 3:12–14. See if you can fill in the blanks below (it's okay to look back at past lessons for help):*

> Therefore, as God's _____ ones, holy and _____ _____ , put on _____ , _____ , _____ , _____ , and _____ , bearing with one another and forgiving one another if anyone has a grievance against another. Just as the Lord has forgiven you, so you are also to forgive. Above all, put on love, which is the perfect bond of unity.

This week we are talking about two things we should put on: forbearance and forgiveness. They are closely tied to each other. You probably already have a good understanding of forgiveness, but what about forbearance? Our verse says we are to "bear with one another," which is what gives us the term "forbearance."

What do you think it means to "bear with" someone?

_____

_____

Our definition of forbearance is: showing self-control when provoked or annoyed. Sometimes people do things that disappoint us or make us angry. Showing forbearance and forgiveness doesn't mean we must like or agree with whatever other people do. But it means we can still love people who do things or live in a way we don't agree with or even do things that the Bible says are wrong.

This week we will learn about a time when Jesus showed forbearance and forgiveness with someone who hurt Him, and we'll learn how He can help us to do the same thing.

Let's thank Him now:

> *Jesus, thank You for bearing with and forgiving people who don't always obey You. Thank You for forgiving me. Help me learn more about forbearance and forgiveness this week, and help me bear with and forgive the people around me. I love You. Amen.*

HE NEVER LEAVES

Before we read today's passage, let's set the scene. Jesus is with His disciples on the night before His death. He knows what is about to happen to Him, and He tells the disciples that they will all "fall away" or leave Him. Let's see what the disciples thought about this.

Read Mark 14:29–31

What does Peter say to Jesus?

_____

_____

Then Jesus says Peter will deny Him _____ *times before the* _____ *crows twice.*

How does Peter respond? Does he agree with Jesus?

_____

_____

Peter and the other disciples had spent the past three years with Jesus. They were like brothers. But Jesus said they would all leave Him. And He went even further and said Peter would *deny* Him.

What does "deny" mean?

_____

How would you feel if one of your friends said they didn't know you and they weren't friends with you?

_____

_____

Peter says he will never deny Jesus, even if it means he has to die with Jesus. Tomorrow we'll find out what Peter did.

Jesus said His friends would all leave Him, but later He would tell them that He would never leave them or forsake them. After He died and rose again, Jesus was about to go back to heaven. He said to all His followers, "Remember, I am with you always, to the end of the age" (Matthew 28:20).

While His disciples may have left Him, He would never leave them. And He will never leave us either, if we put our trust in Him.

Let's thank Him for that now:

Jesus, even though people sometimes deny You and wander away from You, You never leave us. Thank You for promising to be with us always and for keeping Your promise. I'm so glad You are with me. Amen.

HE'S NEVER SURPRISED

Yesterday we learned about when Jesus predicted that His disciples would all leave Him. Do you remember which disciple insisted that he would never leave Jesus, even if it meant he had to die? Who was it?

_____

Peter didn't know what was about to happen to Jesus. He couldn't imagine that Jesus would be arrested by a mob, then brought before leaders who would have Him whipped, mocked, and killed. But Jesus knew, and He knew what Peter would do.

When Jesus was arrested, Peter followed Him and hung around in the courtyard while Jesus was being questioned by the high priest.

Read Mark 14:66–68

The high priest's maidservant saw Peter and said, "You also were with Jesus, the man from Nazareth." She recognized him as one of Jesus' disciples.

How does Peter respond to her? Circle the correct statement:

"You're right, I was one of   **OR**   "I don't know what
His followers and friends."   you're talking about."

Read Mark 14:69–71

The maidservant sees Peter again. What does she do?

_____

_____

_____

And again, Peter denies it.

Then the people standing around Peter say again that he is certainly one of the followers of Jesus, and again Peter says he doesn't know Jesus. The Bible even says Peter curses and swears. He is very upset and probably afraid.

How many times did he deny knowing Jesus? _____

Read Mark 14:72

Draw a picture of what happens in this verse:

Do you feel sorry for Peter? Why or why not?

_____

_____

Have you ever imagined how you would respond if there was an emergency? Your family may have plans in place for a house fire or tornado or earthquake so they can do their best to stay safe. But it's one thing to imagine and plan, and it's another thing to actually live it out. Usually, the way we really act is different from what we imagined in certain situations.

I think that's what happened to Peter. He could never have imagined denying Jesus. He was ready to die for Him! But he didn't know what was about to happen and how afraid he was going to feel.

As Peter stood around a fire outside the place where Jesus was being questioned and beaten, he was probably terrified. Why was Jesus letting this happen? They had seen Him do many miracles. Why wasn't He doing one now to save Himself? And what if they did the same thing to Peter? He wanted to be there to see what was happening to Jesus, but he didn't want to be arrested and beaten. So, when the people recognized him and said they had seen him with Jesus, he denied it, growing more fearful and angrier each time. Then, he heard the rooster crow, remembered the words of Jesus, and wept. He had done the very thing he said he would *never* do.

Peter was surprised by what he had done, but Jesus wasn't. He knew Peter would deny Him. But that didn't change the way He loved Peter. We'll learn more about that tomorrow.

Isn't it good to know that Jesus is not surprised when we sin? He never says, "I can't believe you did that!" when we make bad choices. He knows, and He still loves us and forgives us.

Let's thank Him for that now:

Jesus, thank You that You're never surprised and shocked when I disobey You. And You still love me and forgive me. That is such good news. Thank You for showing me mercy. Help me show mercy to others. Amen.

"DO YOU LOVE ME?"

Yesterday we read the sad story of Peter denying Jesus. But the sad thing is never the last thing for those who love Jesus. Let's find out how this story ends.

The verses we're going to read in John are about something that happened after Jesus died and was raised to life again. The disciples were out on the sea in a boat, and they were fishing. They fished all night and didn't catch anything. In the morning, Jesus called to them from the shore, but they didn't know it was Him. He told them to cast their fishing net on the right side of the boat, and they caught so many fish they couldn't even pull them all into the boat!

Then they realized it was Jesus, and He built a fire and invited them to have breakfast with Him. Let's find out what happened after they ate.

Read John 21:15–17

Jesus asks Peter a question three times. What question does He ask?

_____

_____

Each time, Peter says, "Yes." He even gets a little sad that Jesus keeps asking him the same question. But Jesus has a good reason for this.

Do you remember how many times Peter said he didn't know Jesus in the high priest's courtyard? _____

Now, gathered around the campfire, Jesus was giving Peter a chance to exchange that denial for love. For each time Peter had said he didn't know Jesus, he now got to tell Jesus that he loved Him. And not only that, but Jesus was also giving Peter a very important job.

Each time Peter answers and says that he loves Jesus, Jesus responds with an instruction for Peter. Write them below:

Verse 15: "_____ my lambs."

Verse 16: "_____ my sheep."

Verse 17: "_____ my sheep."

Remember when we learned about how Jesus is the Good Shepherd? In these verses, He is giving Peter a huge responsibility—taking care of His sheep! Jesus gave this big job to the man who had denied even knowing Him. And if you read the book of Acts, you'll learn how Peter changed from the guy who fearfully denied Jesus into the guy who boldly preached about Jesus and helped people know about the kingdom of God.

What does this teach you about Jesus?

_____

_____

_____

Jesus was not surprised when Peter denied Him. But He also didn't cast Peter aside and forget him. He bore with Peter's weakness and fear, and He forgave him for denying Him.

No matter what we've done, we're never too bad for Jesus to forgive us. Isn't that great news?!

Let's thank Him now. Pray the following prayer:

Jesus, I've done a lot of bad things, but I'm so glad to know that You can forgive me and that You still have jobs for me to do in Your kingdom. I love You, and I want to serve You. Please help me do that today. Amen.

PUTTING ON FORBEARANCE AND FORGIVENESS

This week we learned about how Jesus bore with and forgave Peter. Sometimes forbearance means knowing that someone might let us down or do something we don't like and still choosing to love them.

Because Jesus was fully human, He experienced real emotions, just like you and me. He was probably very hurt when Peter denied knowing Him. He didn't say to Peter, "It's no big deal. I don't mind." Peter was sad about what he had done because he knew it was wrong. But Jesus forgave and understood Peter's fear. Instead of holding it against Peter, He gave him an important job and made him a leader.

Let's read Levi's story again:

Levi had worked for days on a large LEGO® castle. He placed a sign on his bedroom door that said, "Do Not Enter . . . LEGO Master at work!" He told his little brother, Donovan, not to go in or touch his creation or he would be in big trouble. So, when Levi came back to his room after getting a snack downstairs, he was shocked to discover Donovan standing over his castle, which was broken in several places.

Write an ending for this story based on what you've learned about forbearance and forgiveness this week:

_____

_____

_____

_____

_____

When people hurt us,* it's okay to feel sad and even angry about it. But we can also ask Jesus to help us bear with others and forgive them. We won't do it perfectly, but He did. He knows what it's like to be hurt, and He can help us to show grace to others.

Turn to page 35. It's time to draw another item of clothing on your person.

On today's article of clothing, write "Forbearance and Forgiveness" (if that's too long, you could choose just one of these words.)

Apply it

Talk through these questions with an adult, a sibling, or a friend:

- What have you learned about Jesus from this passage?

- What have you learned about forbearance and forgiveness from this passage? Why is it so hard to bear with others and forgive them?

- What is an area in your life where you are struggling to bear with others or forgive?

Pray about it

Think about a time when you didn't bear with or forgive someone. Tell God about it, ask His forgiveness, and thank Jesus for showing forgiveness and dying for you. Then, ask Him to help you, by the Holy Spirit, to put on forbearance and forgiveness today. Be specific: Ask for help with certain people or situations you're facing. Ask Him to give you an opportunity to put on these things this week.

Practice it

How can you put on forbearance and forgiveness this week? Here are some ideas, but feel free to think of your own!

- Try to recognize when someone is bearing with you or showing forgiveness. Practice asking others to forgive you.

* Remember: If someone is hurting you or treating you badly, you should always talk to a trusted adult about it. Bearing with people does not mean letting them hurt you without consequences.

- When someone does something that makes you angry, walk away and take some deep breaths while asking God to help you to forbear and forgive.

- Ask God for an opportunity to serve others by sharing the good news about Jesus with someone this week. Each person's greatest need is to believe in Jesus for salvation.

PUT ON LOVE

TRUE LOVE

Naomi had loved 5th grade. She and her best friend, Jasmine, were always together, and Naomi had never felt lonely. But 6th grade was different. She and Jasmine had drifted apart over the summer, and now Jasmine had a new best friend. Naomi had tried to talk with her, but Jasmine was always too busy, and her new friend didn't seem to like Naomi. One day in the bathroom, Naomi overheard them laughing and talking about her. She felt hurt and betrayed and wanted to find a way to get back at Jasmine. She knew all of Jasmine's secrets, and she thought about spreading one around at lunch.

Have you ever felt like Naomi? Maybe a friend you were close to started hanging out with someone else more than you. Or maybe someone embarrassed you. What was the situation, and how did you feel?

_____

_____

_____

_____

_____

_____

 **Love**
choosing to act in ways that seek good for others[11]

_____

11. Love in "2 Peter 1:6-7 Commentary," Precept Austin, https://www.preceptaustin.org/2_peter_16-7#love.

We will talk more about Naomi's story later this week. First, let's review our passage. *Below, see if you can list all the things we're supposed to put on:*

1. C _____

2. K _____

3. H _____

4. G _____

5. F _____ & F _____

6. L _____

In the passage from Colossians 3, "love" comes last. But that doesn't mean it's not as important. In fact, you could say it's the *most* important thing we put on.

Circle the words that tell us how important it is: "Above all, put on love, which is the perfect bond of unity."

Why do you think we are to put on love "above all"? Why is love so important?

_____

_____

_____

This week we will learn more about love from the Bible. We know God loves us because the Bible tells us so. It even says that God *is* love (1 John 4:8). We can know what true love is by looking at how He loves us.

Let's thank Him for that love now:

> Father God, thank You for creating me and loving me. You love me so much that You sent Your Son for me. Help me learn more about Your love this week. Help me be thankful for Your amazing love. Amen.

WHAT DO YOU LOVE?

This week we're learning about love. What do you think of when you hear the word "love"?

_____

_____

In English, we have just one word for love. But in other languages, there are different words for different kinds of love. You might have family love, or romantic love, or friendship love. Or sometimes we say "love" about something we really like. For example, "I love volleyball," or "I love puppies," or "I love Brussels sprouts" or "_____

_____" [you fill in the blank].

The love that we're supposed to "put on" in Colossians 3:14 is not a "like" kind of love. The Greek word used by Paul in this verse is *agape* (ah-*gah*-pay), and it's the kind of love Jesus showed us on the cross. It's a love that chooses what is good for other people, even when we don't feel very loving toward them. *Agape* is a love of sacrifice and devotion.

Find John 15:13 in your Bible, and write it below:

_____

_____

_____

When Jesus said this to the disciples, He was telling them how much He loved them (and us!)—so much that He would lay down His life, which means that He would die for us. He says this is the greatest kind of love there is. And this is the kind of love we should have for each other.

It's hard to imagine choosing to show that kind of love to our friends! Tomorrow, we'll read a verse that might make it seem even harder!

But for now, let's stop and thank Jesus for showing *agape* love to us:

> *Jesus, You showed me the greatest kind of love there is. You chose to give up Your life to save me. Thank You so much! Help me choose to show* agape *love to others today. I love You. Amen.*

WHEN WE DON'T FEEL LOVE

Have you ever read a book or watched a movie where someone shows love to an enemy? Draw a picture or write what happened in the story:

In the verse we read yesterday (John 15:13), Jesus said, "No one has greater love than this: to lay down his life for his friends." That's pretty amazing love.

But Jesus didn't just die for His friends.

Find Romans 5:6–8 in your Bible. Read these verses and answer the questions below:

Verse 7 says someone might dare to die for a _____ *person.*

Verse 8 says God proves His love to us. How?

_____

_____

These verses say that some people might choose to die for someone who is really good. But Jesus died for sinners—people who have chosen to go against God's laws.

Who is easier to love? Circle one:

People who are kind to me   **People who are unkind to me**

I think all of us would say it's harder to love people who don't treat us with kindness. But that's the amazing kind of love Jesus has for us, and it's the kind He can help us have for other people.

One of my favorite books is *The Hiding Place*, the true story of a Dutch woman named Corrie ten Boom who was sent to a concentration camp in Germany during World War II because she sacrificed her own safety to help Jewish people who were being treated in terrible ways. Later in her life, she struggled to love and forgive a guard who had worked at the concentration camp. But she remembered something her father had told her: "Whenever we cannot love in the old, human way . . . God can give us the perfect way."[12]

Do you think you have to feel love for someone to choose to love them?

_____

There are times when we don't feel love for someone, and we can't make ourselves love them. Corrie's dad understood this, and he told her to pray and ask God to give her His perfect love for people who are hard to love. After all, Jesus was the only human who has ever loved perfectly. It's amazing that we can ask Him to help us, and He will!

Is there anyone you have trouble loving? Fill their name in the prayer below and take a minute to ask God for help:

God, You love perfectly, but I don't. Sometimes I don't feel love for _____ . I need Your help to love them. Please help me. Give me Your perfect agape love, and help me choose to love them. Thank You for loving me! Amen.

12. Corrie Ten Boom, *The Hiding Place: Young Reader's Edition* (Bloomington, MN: Chosen, 2015), 36.

NEVER GONNA GIVE US UP

Read Romans 8:38–39 below. Cross off all the things that cannot separate us from God's love (death, life, angels, rulers, and so on).

> For I am persuaded that neither death nor life, nor angels nor rulers, nor things present nor things to come, nor powers, nor height nor depth, nor any other created thing will be able to separate us from the love of God that is in Christ Jesus our Lord.

We have learned about God's *agape* love this week. This is the love that motivated Jesus to die for us, even when we were sinners who did not love Him back.

Today, we read the amazing news that *nothing* can separate us from His wonderful love!

Do you ever worry that God will stop loving you—like if you do too many bad things He will decide He doesn't love you anymore?

_____

_____

God has promised us that nothing can separate us from His love. Instead, He shows us all the things we have studied over the past few weeks: compassion, kindness, forgiveness, and more. His love is big enough to keep loving us even on our worst days.

Write this message from today's verse on a notecard or piece of paper, and put it somewhere where you will see it. Try to memorize it over the next few weeks.

> **Nothing will be able to separate us from the love of God that is in Christ Jesus our Lord.**

Doesn't that make you want everyone to know that kind of love? Do you know anyone who might not know that God loves them? Write their name or names below:

_____

_____

_____

_____

_____

Take a minute to pray and ask God to help you to share His love with those people:

Father God, thank You for promising that nothing can separate me from Your love. That is amazing news! I want everyone to know You and Your love. Please help me tell my friends and family about Your love. I need Your help. I love You. Amen.

PUTTING ON LOVE

This week we learned about how Jesus showed us *agape* love, even when we did not love Him. And we learned that nothing can separate us from His love. We also learned that we may not always feel like loving other people, but He can help us choose love.

Let's read Naomi's story again:

Naomi had loved 5th grade. She and her best friend, Jasmine, were always together and Naomi had never felt lonely. But 6th grade was different. She and Jasmine had drifted apart over the summer, and now Jasmine had a new best friend. Naomi had tried to talk with her, but Jasmine was always too busy, and her new friend didn't seem to like Naomi. One day in the bathroom, Naomi overheard them laughing and talking about her. She felt hurt and betrayed and wanted to find a way to get back at Jasmine. She knew all of Jasmine's secrets, and she thought about spreading one around at lunch.

Write an ending for this story based on what you've learned about love this week:

_____

_____

_____

_____

_____

_____

_____

_____

Turn to page 35. It's time to draw the final item of clothing on your person.

On today's article of clothing, write "Love."

Apply it

Talk through these questions with an adult, a sibling, or a friend:

- What have you learned about Jesus this week?

- What have you learned about love? Why is it so hard to love people sometimes?

- How has Jesus shown love to you?

Pray about it

Think of a time when you didn't show love to someone and talk to God about it. Ask His forgiveness and thank Jesus for loving you. Then, ask Him to help you, by the Holy Spirit, to put on love today. Be specific: Ask for help with certain people or situations you're facing. Ask Him to give you an opportunity to put on love this week.

Practice it

How can you put on love this week? Here are some ideas, but feel free to think of your own!

- Pray for someone you have a hard time loving.

- Give money or food to someone in need.

- Help a sibling or another family member with a project.

- Ask God for an opportunity to share the good news about Jesus with someone this week. Each person's greatest need is to believe in Jesus for salvation.

YOUR NEW "CLOTHES"

You did it! You spent eight weeks learning more about what it means to look more like Jesus and find your identity in Him. You now know what to "wear" as a Christian (and what not to wear). It might seem like learning all this should make it super easy to take off the bad stuff and put on the good. But there will still be days when it is really hard. You will have times when you feel angry instead of patient, or when you want to slander someone instead of bearing with them.

Until we are with Jesus face-to-face, we will all struggle with these things. Remember that, if you have trusted Jesus with your life and are part of God's family, you have the Holy Spirit to help you love and follow Jesus. Ask for help each day. (I have to ask for God's help many times every day.)

My biggest prayer is that you finish this study with a greater love for Jesus. He is all the things we want to be and more. And He loves us! What an amazing gift. And that gift isn't just for us to keep to ourselves. Now that you've finished the study, feel free to go back to the "Practice it" sections in each week and continue doing the things that are listed there. That's a perfect way to share the love of Jesus with others!

For your final challenge, see if you can fill in the blanks of Colossians 3:12–14:

Therefore, as _____ chosen ones, _____ and _____
_____ , put on _____ , _____ ,
_____ , _____ , and _____ ,
_____ with one _____ and _____ one
another if anyone has a _____ against another. Just as the
_____ has forgiven you, so you are also to _____ .
Above ____ , put on _____ , which is the perfect bond of _____ .

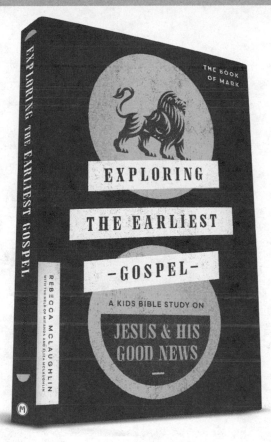

More Books Kids Love
and Parents Trust

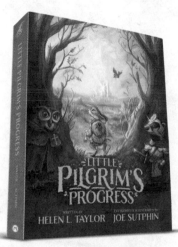